HIKING IN FR

A Comprehensive Hiking Guide to Explore Iconic Trails in France - (The French Alps, Pyrenees, Coastal Trails, and Wine Country)

CURZIO MANNA

CONTENTS

INTRODUCTION

Hiking in France: A Quick Overview

France, known for its rich history, fine gastronomy, and breathtaking scenery, is also a hiking paradise. Hiking possibilities abound, ranging from the magnificent Alps and the rough Pyrenees to attractive seaside walks and green wine region trails. Hiking is more than just a physical exercise in France;

it is a holistic experience that mixes natural beauty with cultural inquiry.

With its snow-capped peaks and beautiful lakes, the French Alps draw travelers looking for tough paths and stunning landscapes. The Mont Blanc Circuit, the Alps' crown jewel, leads hikers around Western Europe's highest mountain, providing a unique alpine experience. The GR20 track in Corsica, known as Europe's hardest long-distance trail, offers a unique combination of coastal scenery and rocky terrain.

The Pyrenees provide a distinct but equally compelling trip for those attracted to the boundary between France and Spain. For experienced hikers, the Haute Route, which traverses high mountain passes, delivers a hard but rewarding journey. Exploring the Pyrenean National Park reveals unspoiled environment, unique flora and animals, and a humbling and energizing feeling of seclusion.

The coastal areas of France have a certain appeal. The Brittany Coastal Path, also known as the GR34, passes past magnificent cliffs, sandy beaches, and attractive fishing communities. Calanques National Park, located near Marseille, has crystal-clear Mediterranean seas and magnificent limestone cliffs, making for an ideal combination of trekking and beach exploration.

Hiking among vineyards is extremely popular among wine connoisseurs. Hiking through picturesque towns and rolling vine-covered hills on the Alsace Wine Route, while the Beaujolais Vineyards give a sensory experience through the aromatic grapevines.

The Goal of the Guide

The goal of this thorough book is to be a trustworthy and knowledgeable companion for anybody looking to experience the fascinating world of hiking in France. This book is designed to give critical insights, practical guidance, and inspiration, whether you're a seasoned hiker searching for new challenges or a newbie ready to go on your first hiking experience.

First and foremost, this book is intended to serve as a doorway for walkers into France's different landscapes. It encourages hikers to make educated decisions based on their tastes and skills by providing thorough information about numerous routes, including difficulty ratings, trail highlights, and suggested seasons. The guide delves into the cultural and historical importance of each place, offering a comprehensive insight of the surroundings.

Furthermore, this book is intended to meet the demands of a diverse audience. Whether you like tough high-altitude excursions, peaceful beach walks, or cultural tours through wineries, the book has something for everyone. It also takes into account different levels of competence, providing suggestions for both novice and experienced hikers, ensuring that everyone can choose a path that matches their ability level and interests.

The tour encourages appropriate and sustainable hiking methods in addition to showing the beauty of the trails. It encourages environmental awareness and appropriate connections with local people by encouraging a Leave No Trace mentality. The guide hopes to help to the preservation of these spectacular settings for future generations by instilling a feeling of respect for environment and cultural heritage.

Target Audience

This book is written for a wide range of hiking enthusiasts, from beginners looking to take their first steps on the route to seasoned hikers looking for new challenges. The intended audience consists of:

a. Beginner Hikers: People who are new to hiking and want to find accessible paths with intermediate difficulty levels and beautiful scenery. For a good first hiking experience, the book gives crucial information on gear, safety, and easy-to-follow pathways.

b. Intermediate Hikers: Hikers with some hiking experience looking for more difficult hikes and various sceneries. The book provides thorough information on moderate to tough walks, enabling intermediate hikers to broaden their repertory and challenge their limits.

c. Seasoned Hikers looking for challenging treks, off-the-beaten-path activities, and in-depth cultural discovery. For a completely immersive experience, the book includes information on difficult routes, high-altitude climbs, and less-traveled places.

d. Cultural Explorers: People who want to combine hiking with cultural activities like visiting wineries, historical monuments, and lovely towns. The book contains sections on each region's cultural and historical importance, appealing to individuals who value a well-rounded travel experience.

e. Environmentally Conscious Travelers: Hikers who stress ethical and sustainable behaviors are known as environmentally conscious travelers. The handbook emphasizes Leave No Trace ideals, environmental awareness, and cultural respect, appealing to individuals who desire to leave as little of an influence on the natural and cultural legacy of the areas they visit.

The guide aspires to be an inclusive and beneficial resource for everyone looking to start on a great hiking journey in France's beautiful landscapes by addressing the different requirements and interests of this target audience.

GENERAL INFORMATION FOR YOUR HIKING TRIP

Geographic Overview

France's geographic variety is a treasure trove for walkers, with scenery to suit every taste and ability level. The country's landscape is a canvas of natural treasures waiting to be discovered, from the undulating hills of the countryside to the towering peaks of mountain ranges.

a. Landscape Varieties

France has an incredible range of landscapes, each with its own distinct appeal. Vineyards, orchards, and meadows decorate the landscape, while deep woods offer a shelter for nature enthusiasts. The Jura Mountains contrast with the lavender meadows of Provence with their clean lakes and lush woods. The Causses' limestone plateaus produce a bizarre landscape riddled with deep canyons and caverns.

With their craggy cliffs, sandy beaches, and scenic coves, coastal locations add to this variety. The turquoise seas of the Mediterranean coast stand in sharp contrast to the rugged and untamed beauty of the Atlantic shore. Exploring these distinct landscapes is like traveling through several planets inside the confines of a same nation.

b. Mountain Ranges

The Alps and Pyrenees, France's renowned mountain ranges, provide a playground for hikers seeking both adventure and calm.

With their towering peaks, glaciers, and alpine meadows, the French Alps provide a stunning background for daring journeys. The tallest summit in Western Europe, Mont Blanc, invites climbers and hikers alike, while the Vanoise National Park offers a wildlife refuge among breathtaking surroundings.

The Pyrenees constitute a natural barrier between France and Spain on the southern border. This mountainous mountain range is home to a variety of habitats, ranging from verdant valleys to high-altitude plateaus. Hiking along the GR10 or the aforementioned Haute Route enables travelers to cross these spectacular peaks while also experiencing the region's distinct cultural mix.

c. Coastal Areas
Hikers may discover the meeting point of land and water along France's coastline, which is a tapestry of magnificent splendor. The Brittany Coastal Path (GR34) travels

along the craggy cliffs and sandy beaches of Brittany, offering spectacular views of the Atlantic Ocean. Calanques National Park, located near Marseille, exhibits the Mediterranean's crystalline seas, secret coves, and limestone cliffs, providing a stark contrast to the northern coastlines.

Coastal hiking not only offers spectacular views but also cultural immersion, with lovely fishing communities, antique lighthouses, and marine customs dotting the coastline. The mix of coastal and inland trekking guarantees that France's beauty goes beyond its interior to its enthralling coasts.

Climate Considerations
Understanding the weather is essential for planning a great hike in France. The nation has a wide variety of climates, which are impacted by its physical characteristics and closeness to various bodies of water.

a. Seasonal Changes

France has four different seasons, each with its own particular environment for hikers. Spring (March to May) ushers in blossoming wildflowers, mild weather, and lush green sceneries. Summer (June to August) is the best time to visit, with pleasant weather excellent for mountain treks and beach excursions. Autumn (September to November) paints the landscapes with rich crimson and gold colors, making for a beautiful background for trekking. Winter (December to February) draws snow lovers to the Alps' snow-covered paths.

Hikers must take these seasonal fluctuations into account when planning their journeys. Spring and fall have warmer temperatures and less people, making them ideal for individuals looking for a more peaceful experience.

b. Best Hiking Seasons

The optimum time to hike in France is determined primarily on the area and the sort of experience you desire. Summer is good for high-altitude walks in the Alps, while seaside paths are appealing in the summer. The seasons of spring and fall are ideal for exploring vineyard paths and historical pathways.

Hikers looking for snow-covered landscapes and winter activities might arrange winter visits to the Alps. Check individual trail conditions, since certain routes may be restricted or difficult during certain seasons. Additionally, popular trails may encounter increased traffic in the summer, so visitors looking for a more peaceful experience may want to come during the shoulder seasons.

Historical and Cultural Importance

Hiking routes in France are not just walks through nature, but also excursions through history and culture. The paths wind through landscapes that have seen millennia of human activity, allowing hikers to interact with the country's rich cultural and historical fabric.

a. Historical Routes & Trails

France is riddled with paths that give evidence to the country's historical history. The Chemin de St-Jacques (Way of St. James) is a medieval pilgrimage road in Spain that leads to the ancient city of Santiago de Compostela. This path not only provides a physical challenge, but it also immerses trekkers in the pilgrimage's spiritual and cultural importance.

Another historical treasure is the Sentier Cathare (Cathar Trail), which travels across the Pyrenees foothills, past medieval castles and old remains. Hiking this walk is like taking a step back in time, discovering the places where historical events took place.

b. Cultural Encounters Along the Trails

Hiking in France is about more than simply the landscape; it's also about engaging with the local culture. Hikers may tour picturesque towns, drink local wines, and learn about winemaking traditions handed down through centuries along the Alsace Wine Route.

The Provence paths allow visitors to immerse themselves in the region's creative legacy, with vistas that inspired legendary artists such as Cézanne and Van Gogh. The GR34 trail along the Brittany coast introduces hikers to the marine culture, including seafood festivals, lighthouses, and traditional Breton music.

Hiking, in essence, transforms into a cultural excursion, connecting hikers with the customs, stories, and people that have influenced the places they pass through. The trails of France provide a diversified cultural experience, whether it's meeting local artists, attending festivals, or staying in medieval towns.

Finally, the geographic, climatic, cultural, and historical components of hiking in France weave a tapestry of experiences for outdoor lovers. Each factor, from the varied scenery to the seasonal differences, adds to the attractiveness of trekking in this enchanting nation. The trails not only present physical obstacles, but also a glimpse into France's cultural and historical spirit, making each stride a voyage across time and landscape.

ESSENTIAL PLANNING

Entry Requirements

A hike in France requires careful consideration of visa and admission restrictions. A Schengen visa is required for citizens of numerous countries to enter France. Check the exact visa requirements depending on your nationality and the length of your stay. The following are important aspects to remember:

a. Visa for the Schengen Area

Make sure you apply for your Schengen visa well in advance of your trip. This visa grants you access to the Schengen Area, which includes France. Provide any relevant documentation, such as evidence of lodging, travel insurance, and a comprehensive itinerary outlining your hiking objectives.

b. Stay Duration

Understand the visa's permitted term of stay. Hiking trips, particularly those covering long-distance trails, may last longer than the average tourist trip, so plan accordingly.

c. Specific Area Permits

Some hiking areas in France may have permit requirements. Investigate the trails you intend to visit and check for any additional permits or restrictions.

d. Visa Extensions

Inquire about visa extensions if you intend to extend your stay for additional hiking or travel. It should be noted that extensions may have specific criteria and must be requested before the original visa expires.

e. Entry Points
Determine the entry points through which you can enter France with your Schengen visa. Consider the ease of access in relation to your hiking itinerary.

Remember that visa requirements can change, so for the most up-to-date information, always consult the official government websites or the French embassy in your country.

Safety and Health
When embarking on a hiking adventure in France, it is critical to ensure your health and safety. From vaccinations to emergency services, meticulous planning is required.

a. Vaccinations
Check and update routine vaccinations to prioritize your health. Additionally, consider vaccinations or boosters for specific diseases

based on your travel plans. Consult with your healthcare provider to ensure you are adequately protected against illnesses such as tetanus, hepatitis A and B, and tick-borne encephalitis, especially if your hiking trails take you through wooded areas.

b. Emergency Services
Familiarize yourself with emergency services and healthcare facilities along your hiking route. Save important contact numbers, including local emergency services and the nearest hospital, in your phone and on a printed copy. The European Emergency Number (similar to 911) is 112, and it can be dialed for assistance in any EU country.

Carry a basic first aid kit that includes items like bandages, antiseptic wipes, pain relievers, and any personal medications. Knowing basic first aid skills is also advantageous for any unforeseen situations on the trail.

In remote areas, consider a personal locator beacon (PLB) or satellite communication device to request assistance in case of emergencies.

Currency and Money Matters

Understanding the currency, managing finances, and being aware of payment methods are vital aspects of planning for a hiking trip in France.

a. Currency Exchange

The official currency in France is the Euro (EUR). Before your trip, exchange currency at a reliable source, such as banks or currency exchange offices. It's advisable to carry some cash for smaller establishments and remote areas where card acceptance may be limited.

b. Credit and Debit Cards

Credit and debit cards are widely accepted in urban areas and popular tourist destinations. Notify your bank about your travel dates to avoid any issues with card transactions. Check for any foreign transaction fees or inform your bank of your travel plans to ensure uninterrupted card usage.

c. ATMs
ATMs are readily available in cities and towns. Withdraw cash as needed but be cautious of withdrawal fees. Inform your bank about your travel dates and destination to avoid any potential issues with ATM transactions.

d. Budgeting
Plan your budget for the hiking trip, considering accommodation, meals, transportation, and any park or trail fees. Research the cost of living in the areas you'll be visiting and plan accordingly.

e. Trail Services
Some long-distance hiking trails may have limited access to banking services. Plan for this by carrying sufficient cash for expenses

along the trail, such as accommodation in mountain huts or refuges.

Language Considerations

Navigating language differences is an integral part of preparing for a hiking trip in France. While French is the official language, there are considerations to make communication smoother during your adventure.

a. Basic French Phrases:

While English is commonly spoken in tourist areas, especially in larger cities, making an effort to speak French is not only courteous but can also enhance your overall experience. Here are some essential phrases to have in your linguistic toolkit:

Greetings:

- Bonjour (Hello / Good morning)
- Bonsoir (Good evening)
- Bonne nuit (Good night)

Polite Expressions:

- Merci (Thank you)
- S'il vous plaît (Please)
- Excusez-moi (Excuse me / I'm sorry)

Directions and Location:

- Où est... ? (Where is...?)
- À droite (To the right)
- À gauche (To the left)

Common Questions:

- Comment ça va ? (How are you?)
- Combien ça coûte ? (How much does it cost?)
- Parlez-vous anglais ? (Do you speak English?)

Emergency Phrases:

- Aidez-moi (Help me)
- J'ai besoin d'aide (I need help)

- Numéro d'urgence (Emergency number)

b. Apps for Language Learning
Language applications might be a convenient method to get acquainted with French before your trip. These applications include interactive lessons and activities that can help you improve your vocabulary, pronunciation, and understanding. Here are some noteworthy language apps:

- **Duolingo:** This program gamifies language learning, making it more entertaining and effective.
- **Babbel** focuses on communication skills, assisting you in learning useful words for everyday circumstances.
- **Rosetta Stone:** Known for its immersive approach, Rosetta Stone assists learners in thinking in the language they are learning.

c. Offline Translation Apps

An offline translation tool may be quite useful in locations with restricted internet availability. You may use Google Translate without an internet connection by downloading language packs that enable you to translate text or utilize the camera for real-time translation.

d. Dialects of the Region

Understanding fundamental phrases in local dialects or languages may serve as a cultural bridge in places with unique local dialects or languages, particularly in rural areas. While not required, it indicates a respect for the local history. Locals often appreciate tourists who make an attempt to converse in their language.

e. Cultural Awareness

It is critical to approach linguistic disparities with cultural awareness. Even if it's only a few simple words, French people, especially in smaller towns and villages, may appreciate your attempt to speak their language. It promotes pleasant connection and shows respect for the local culture.

Remember that the aim is successful communication and cultural interaction, not fluency. Even learning and utilizing a few words may substantially improve your relationship with the local people and enrich your hiking trip in France.

Transportation

Planning transportation for your hiking vacation in France entails both traveling to the country and properly navigating local transit alternatives. Let's take a closer look at these points:

a. How to Get to France

Flights:
Plan ahead of time to research and book flights. Charles de Gaulle Airport in Paris, Nice Côte d'Azur Airport, and Lyon-Saint Exupéry Airport are among France's major international airports. Consider the airports'

closeness to your hike starting place and make your selection appropriately.

Entry Points:
Determine the best entry points depending on your trip schedule. If you're starting your walk in the Alps, traveling into Geneva, Switzerland, could be a good idea. Similarly, if you're planning a trip to the Pyrenees, airports in Toulouse or Barcelona (Spain) may be acceptable.

Airport Ground Transportation:
Plan your transportation from the airport to your starting spot. The rail network in France is broad and efficient, and major airports are well-connected to train terminals. Consider taking the train to your hiking location for a lovely excursion.

b. Local Transportation Options

Trains:
The SNCF train system in France is one of the greatest ways to visit the nation.

Regional trains serve smaller communities while high-speed trains link big cities. Consider taking a train to the trailhead if you're going hiking.

Buses:
Regional and long-distance buses are inexpensive ways to travel between cities and communities. They are especially handy for getting to trailheads in more isolated places that are not readily accessible by train.

Rental Cars:
Renting a vehicle may be a practical choice if your hiking schedule involves visiting remote or less accessible locations. It gives you freedom and enables you to reach trailheads that are not easily accessible by public transit.

Local Transportation Apps:
For short-distance travel inside cities or to and from trailheads, use transportation apps like Uber or local taxi services. For longer

trips, apps like BlaBlaCar provide ridesharing choices.

Shuttles and Transfers for Hiking:
Shuttle services or scheduled transports to trailheads may be available in popular hiking areas. Investigate these choices ahead of time, particularly for long-distance treks where logistics might be more complicated.

Biking:
Renting a bike may be a sustainable and entertaining way to explore the countryside and access trailheads in certain areas, especially those with well-developed cycling infrastructure.

Carefully planning your transportation provides a smooth transition from your arrival in France to the start of your hiking excursion. It also helps you to maximize your time on the trails by eliminating extra logistical hurdles.

Do you want additional information about a certain mode of transportation or advice for navigating local transit, or do you want to go to the next section?

TOP HIKING LOCATIONS

Hiking in France means seeing some of the country's most renowned and attractive locations. From the towering Alps to the rough grandeur of the Pyrenees, each location provides a one-of-a-kind and memorable experience. Let's have a look at the best hiking spots in France:

The Alps in France

With their towering peaks, pure lakes, and dramatic landscapes, the French Alps are an iconic destination for hikers looking for both difficulty and stunning views. Here is a comprehensive look at everything the French Alps have to offer:

a. Mont Blanc Tour

The Mont Blanc Circuit is the crown gem of the French Alps, luring hikers with unrivaled alpine splendor. This legendary path circumnavigates Mont Blanc, Western Europe's highest summit, carrying explorers through France, Italy, and Switzerland. The 170-kilometer route takes hikers over high mountain passes, lush valleys, and lovely alpine communities.

From crossing glaciers to traversing alpine meadows decorated with bright wildflowers, the path provides a broad variety of experiences. Hikers are rewarded with magnificent vistas of the Mont Blanc massif, an awe-inspiring panorama of towering peaks and seracs, as they rise.

Rustic mountain cottages and refuges along the route give shelter and a unique chance to interact with other hikers. The camaraderie among hikers, exchanging tales and experiences in these high-altitude refuges, gives the Mont Blanc Circuit a social component.

Because the circuit contains hard stretches with steep ascents and descents, hiking the Mont Blanc Circuit demands a decent degree of fitness and mountain trekking expertise. The benefits, on the other hand, are immense, ranging from the feeling of success that comes with completing the circuit to unforgettable recollections of alpine splendor.

b. The Corsican GR20

The GR20 in Corsica offers a thrilling chance for those looking for a more strenuous and adventurous walk. The GR20, known as one of Europe's most difficult long-distance paths, crosses the island's jagged spine, sending hikers through different environments ranging from steep summits to lush woods.

The path is around 180 kilometers long and is known for its difficult terrain, including portions with via ferrata components. Hikers must negotiate narrow slopes, ascents and descents, and are rewarded with stunning views of the Corsican Alps and the Mediterranean Sea.

The GR20 is a physical challenge as well as an immersion into Corsican culture. Hikers pass through mountain refuges that serve basic but substantial meals, giving them a taste of the local cuisine. The camaraderie among trekkers is evident, fostering a feeling of community as everyone participates in the trail's hardships and achievements.

Corsica's distinct combination of French and Italian cultures provides a cultural dimension to the trekking experience. The GR20 is an expedition that pushes the boundaries while providing a true tour of Corsica's wild beauty.

Finally, the French Alps, particularly the Mont Blanc Circuit and the GR20 in Corsica, offer hikers a twin promise: the beauty of towering peaks and the difficulty of difficult terrain. These routes, each with its own distinct personality, capture the spirit of alpine adventure and leave an unforgettable impact on those who dare to follow them.

The Pyrenees Mountain Range
The Pyrenees, located between France and Spain, provide an intriguing combination of harsh landscapes, ancient paths, and cultural

variety. Let's have a look at the hiking opportunities in the Pyrenees:

a. The Haute Route

The Pyrenees Haute Route is a traditional long-distance walk that traverses the whole mountain range, delivering an epic adventure from the Atlantic to the Mediterranean Sea. This track provides a unique combination of difficult ascents, peaceful valleys, and cultural discovery.

Hikers begin in the Basque Country on the Atlantic coast and make their way to the Mediterranean over steep mountain passes, deep woods, and charming towns. The path highlights the Pyrenees' various ecosystems, from the lush vegetation of the western slopes to the barren landscapes of the eastern portions.

The Haute Route is more than just a physical challenge; it's a chance to immerse oneself in the region's rich cultural tapestry. Hikers meet old churches, medieval castles, and typical mountain communities along the journey, affording a look into the Pyrenees' historical past.

The path is usually separated into phases, enabling hikers to tailor their experience according to their time and tastes. The Haute Route provides a broad range of experiences, whether conquering difficult high-altitude mountains or appreciating the tranquillity of pastoral surroundings.

b. Hiking in the Pyrenean National Park

Pyrenean National Park is a pristine environment ready to be found for anyone looking for a more concentrated study of the Pyrenees. This national park, located in the heart of the mountain range, is a paradise for nature lovers.

The Pyrenean National Park's hiking paths wind through lush valleys, alpine meadows, and along crystal-clear mountain streams. The park is home to a variety of species, including marmots, chamois, and golden eagles, and provides hikers with the opportunity to experience the natural beauty and richness of the Pyrenean environment.

The possibility to walk to high-altitude lakes surrounded by breathtaking mountain vistas is one of the pleasures of trekking in the Pyrenean National Park. The Lac de Gaube, for example, is a beautiful glacial lake accessible by a picturesque walk that offers a tranquil atmosphere for thought and enjoyment of the surrounding scenery.

In essence, the Pyrenees entice hikers with a mix of difficult long-distance paths and peaceful national park exploration. From the Basque Country to the Mediterranean, the region's cultural and ecological richness guarantees that every step is a discovery, making the Pyrenees an amazing hiking destination.

Coastal Trails

The coastline of France is an enthralling patchwork of cliffs, beaches, and turquoise seas. Hiking coastal pathways provides hikers with a unique view of where land meets water. Let's look at two popular beach hikes: the GR34 in Brittany and the Calanques National Park in Marseille.

a. Brittany Coastal Path (GR34)

The GR34, commonly known as the Brittany Coastal Path, is a captivating route that travels around the region's craggy cliffs and sandy beaches. Hikers may immerse themselves in the raw splendor of the Atlantic Ocean at this coastal jewel.

The GR34 traverses the Brittany coastline, beginning at the lovely town of Le Conquet and offering stunning views of the sea and ever-changing scenery. Hikers go through heathlands, dunes, and secluded coves, marveling at the stark contrast of jagged cliffs against the expanse of the ocean.

The path travels through lovely fishing communities like Ploumanac'h and Perros-Guirec, where hikers may learn about Brittany's marine culture. The seaside route is enhanced by traditional Breton buildings, lighthouses, and the rhythmic sound of waves.

Coastal trekking gives not just physical exertion but also opportunities for thought as you gaze out at the expanse of the ocean. Sunsets on the GR34 are a sight to see, throwing a warm light over the coastal landscapes and leaving an unforgettable imprint on those who embark on this marine experience.

b. Calanques National Park

Calanques National Park, located near Marseille, provides a unique coastal experience, distinguished by limestone cliffs, secret bays, and the crystalline seas of the Mediterranean. Hiking routes in this park lead visitors through a scenery that contrasts rocky topography with the turquoise splendor of the sea.

The Calanques, or small inlets with high, limestone cliffs, are the park's distinguishing characteristic. Hiking along pathways like the well-known Calanques En Vau trail enables you to uncover these hidden beauties. The hike's reward is a hidden

Calanque with turquoise waters, ideal for a refreshing dip.

Calanques National Park is a refuge for hikers as well as wildlife enthusiasts. The park is home to a wide range of coastal-adapted vegetation and animals. A sensory-rich hiking experience is created by the aromas of Mediterranean plants, the sound of cicadas, and the panoramic vistas of the sea.

Coastal paths in France provide a dynamic and engaging adventure where hikers may experience the natural beauty of the coastline and interact with the areas' marine history. The GR34 in Brittany and the Calanques National Park are two examples of different coastal attractions that invite travelers to discover the meeting point of land and water.

Hiking in the Wine Country

Not only is France's wine area famous for its vineyards and winemaking traditions, but it also has beautiful paths that run through stunning landscapes. Let's take a look at two popular wine country hikes: the Alsace Wine Route and the Beaujolais Vineyards.

a. The Wine Route of Alsace

The Alsace Wine Route takes you through vineyard-covered slopes, quaint towns, and centuries-old winemaking traditions. This route provides a sensory immersion into the world of Alsace wines, as well as the region's stunning landscape.

The Alsace Wine Route, which runs from Marlenheim to Thann, brings walkers through vineyards that produce some of the world's best white wines. Against the background of the Vosges Mountains, the carefully placed rows of grapevines form a patchwork of hues.

Hikers may visit charming villages such as Riquewihr and Eguisheim, which have half-timbered buildings that ooze medieval beauty. Along the way, wine cellars invite walkers to sample the tastes of Alsace wines such as the famed Riesling and Gewürztraminer.

The route not only highlights the natural beauty of the wine valley, but it also provides insight into the winemaking process. Along the way, interpretive signs explain grape types, vineyard management, and the cultural importance of wine in Alsace.

b. Vineyards in Beaujolais

Hikers are invited to experience the undulating landscapes and sun-kissed vineyards of the Beaujolais area, which is noted for its vivid and delicious Gamay wines. Hiking through the Beaujolais Vineyards is a sensory experience, with odors of ripening grapes mingling with earthy scents of the countryside.

Trails crisscross the area, taking hikers into the heart of Beaujolais and passing through picturesque towns like Fleurie and Morgon. These routes provide panoramic views of the vine-covered slopes, making them a visual feast for both wine fans and nature lovers.

In Beaujolais, harvest season, which occurs in September, lends an added element of excitement to the trekking experience. As grape pickers harvest the bunches that will be converted into the region's famed Beaujolais Nouveau, the vineyards come alive with activity.

Hiking in the Beaujolais Vineyards is a celebration of terroir, the specific blend of soil, climate, and human artistry that gives Beaujolais wines their distinct flavor.

Finally, wine country trekking in France provides a beautiful blend of natural beauty, cultural legacy, and, of course, the pleasure of sampling outstanding wines. Hikers may immerse themselves in the Alsace Wine Route and the Beaujolais Vineyards, where every step is a celebration of the rich viticultural traditions that have formed these famous wine areas.

These best hiking spots provide a taste of the different landscapes and experiences available in France. Whether you're looking for the challenge of high mountain passes, the serenity of seaside routes, or the cultural richness of wine country, each location guarantees a memorable and enjoyable hiking journey.

TRAIL DIFFICULTY LEVELS

Easy Trails for Beginners

Hiking is a wonderful experience, and simple paths provide the ideal introduction for novices to appreciate the beauty of nature without overpowering obstacles. Here's a thorough look at several simple hikes designed for individuals taking their initial steps into the world of hiking:

a. Trail Characteristics

Easy trails are distinguished by well-kept, flat routes that lead novices through scenic surroundings. These pathways often meander through meadows, forests, or beside tranquil bodies of water, giving a relaxing and delightful trek. The emphasis is on creating a good and approachable outdoor experience.

b. Duration and Distance

Easy trails are shorter in length, often ranging from 1 to 5 kilometers. This enables novices to finish the trek in a few hours comfortably, promoting a feeling of success without physical strain. The focus is on having fun and gaining confidence.

c. Accessibility
Easy paths are welcoming and accessible to a diverse variety of people, making them perfect for families with children or those with minimal hiking experience. Many of these routes are wheelchair accessible, ensuring that everyone may enjoy the thrill of outdoor adventure.

d. Safety Considerations
While easy trails may seem to be simple, safety is always a top consideration. Water, food, a route map, and a basic first aid pack are all recommended for beginners. Proper footwear and weather-appropriate gear are important factors in ensuring a safe and enjoyable hiking experience.

e. Easy Trails in France to Try

- Gorges du Fier, Haute-Savoie: A charming route with wooden walks across a tiny canyon that is appropriate for all ages.

- Lac de Servières, Auvergne: An simple loop around a picturesque alpine lake with wonderful views and no difficult terrain.

Easy routes introduce newcomers to the joys of hiking, cultivating a love of the outdoors and building the groundwork for future experiences.

Moderate Trails for Intermediate Hikers

After gaining comfort on simple routes, intermediate hikers typically desire a little more difficulty and diversity in their hiking experiences. Moderate routes provide a mix between accessibility and adventure, making them a great step for those wishing to broaden their horizons. Here's an in-depth look at several moderate paths designed for intermediate hikers:

a. Terrain Variation

Moderate trails provide a variety of topography, such as gradual ascents and descents, as well as some uneven surfaces. Hikers may come across rocky trails, exposed roots, or steeper parts, giving a layer of variation to the trip.

b. Distance and Duration

Moderate trails have a larger variety of lengths, often ranging from 5 to 10 miles. Hiking lengths may range from a half-day to a full day, providing a more immersive experience while still being accessible for individuals with moderate fitness levels.

c. Elevation Gain

Moderate paths, although not as difficult as advanced trails, may require considerable elevation rise. This might include hills or low mountainous places, which allow hikers to improve their cardiovascular fitness while also enjoying lofty views.

d. Scenic Benefits

Intermediate paths often lead to visual highlights such as overlooks, waterfalls, or mountain panoramas. These natural attractions inspire hikers to take on modest difficulties and enjoy the beauty of the outdoors.

e. Moderate Trails in France to Consider

- Cirque de Gavarnie, Pyrenees: A moderate circle hike with spectacular views of Gavarnie Falls and neighboring peaks.
- Sentier des Ocres, Provence: A modest trek among colorful ocher cliffs with unusual geological characteristics.

Intermediate paths provide a more immersive experience while increasing stamina and confidence for hikers advancing from simple routes.

Challenging Trails for Experienced Hikers

Experienced hikers prefer paths that test them physically and emotionally. The excitement of overcoming daunting environments is provided by challenging paths, which need a greater degree of ability and stamina. Here's a thorough examination of difficult paths geared for hikers with substantial hiking experience:

a. Technical Difficulty and Terrain

Challenging paths often have varied and difficult terrain. Steep ascents and descents, rocky scrambles, exposed ridges, and perhaps alpine settings are all possibilities. Technical components like as boulder fields or parts with fixed ropes may be present, necessitating hikers' ability to navigate complicated environments.

b. Distance and Duration

Trails that cover significant lengths often vary from 10 to 20 miles or more. Hiking trips may last many days, needing careful preparation and consideration of aspects such as weather and daylight. These treks are a test of endurance and need a dedication to prolonged physical activity.

c. High Altitude and Elevation Gain

Hiking on difficult terrain sometimes involves substantial elevation increase, leading hikers to mountain peaks or high-altitude situations. Altitude-related difficulties, such as thin air and quick weather changes, add another degree of complication. Acclimatization and understanding of altitude-related concerns are critical for safety.

d. Wilderness Experience

Many difficult treks pass through distant and less-traveled places, providing an authentic wilderness experience. Hikers should be self-sufficient, carrying all required equipment and supplies, and have backcountry skills including navigation, water purification, and Leave No Trace principles.

e. Risk Management

Challenging paths are naturally more dangerous. Hikers must be skilled at identifying and reducing the dangers involved with tough terrain, changeable weather, and possible crises. It is critical to have vital safety items on hand, such as a first aid pack and communication devices.

f. Challenging Trails in France to Try:

- The Tour du Mont Blanc (TMB) is a traditional and difficult multi-day walk that circumnavigates Mont Blanc, passing through France, Italy, and Switzerland.
- Corsica's GR20 track is renowned as one of Europe's most difficult long-distance trails, traversing rough hilly terrain and providing beautiful views of Corsica.

Challenging paths put a hiker's abilities, stamina, and sense of adventure to the test. They provide incomparable natural beauty as well as the feeling of satisfaction that comes from overcoming daunting environments.

Multi-Day Hikes Recommendations

Multi-day treks provide a unique chance to immerse oneself in the outdoors for those wanting prolonged backcountry experiences and a deeper connection with nature. Here's an in-depth look at multi-day hike options for hikers wishing to go on remarkable adventures:

a. Trail Choice

Multi-day walks allow you to see different areas and cover more territory. The trails used for multi-day expeditions should be well-established, with access to water sources and camping spots. Popular long-distance paths often have dedicated shelters or campsites.

b. Essential Backpacking Gear

Hikers going on multi-day treks must carefully pick and pack their equipment. A dependable backpack, lightweight tent, sleeping bag, and cooking supplies are required. Food that is lightweight, compact, and nutritionally packed is essential for maintaining energy over long periods of time.

c. Navigation and Planning

Planning is essential for multi-day treks. Hikers should plan their routes carefully, taking into account daily miles, height increase, and probable camping places. For remaining on track, topographic maps, a compass, and understanding of navigation procedures are vital, particularly on less-marked paths.

d. Physical and Mental Fitness

Multi-day walks need a greater degree of physical condition as well as mental fortitude. Hikers should be prepared to hike for many days in a row, frequently with a heavy rucksack. Mental toughness is essential, particularly during difficult stretches or in severe weather conditions.

e. Leave No Trace Principles

Practicing Leave No Trace principles is especially important on multi-day walks. Natural places may be preserved by minimizing environmental damage, packing away all rubbish, and protecting animal habitats.

f. Recommendation for a Multi-Day Hike in France

The Pyrenees' GR10 provides a demanding and rewarding multi-day adventure across different landscapes, stretching about 538 kilometers from the Atlantic to the Mediterranean.

g. Safety Considerations

Hikers who want to walk for many days should emphasize safety. It is critical to have a full first aid equipment, communication devices, and knowledge of emergency protocols on hand. It is important to check weather predictions and be prepared for changing circumstances in order to have a safe and pleasurable trip.

Multi-day treks are a transforming trip that allows hikers to disengage from the rush and bustle of everyday life and immerse themselves in nature's rhythms. These experiences instill a profound love of the nature and leave enduring memories.

Finally, each trail difficulty level caters to a distinct stage in a hiker's journey, offering individualized experiences that fit with skill levels and ambitions. The trails of France beckon outdoor enthusiasts to embark on a journey of exploration, self-discovery, and adventure, whether it's the gentle embrace of easy trails for beginners, the varied landscapes of moderate trails for intermediate hikers, the rugged challenges of experienced hikers on challenging trails, or the immersive wilderness experience of multi-day hikes.

GEAR AND PACKING

Required Equipment Checklist

Whether you're going on a short day walk or a multi-day backcountry trip, having the correct gear is essential for comfort, safety, and pleasure. Here is a thorough list of necessary hiking gear that every hiker should consider:

a. Navigation:

- Map of the topography

- Compass
- Optional GPS unit

b. Shelter:

- Tent (suitable for multi-day treks)
- Sleeping Bag
- Sleeping Pad

c. Clothing:

- Base layers that wick away moisture
- Layers of insulation
- The outer layers are waterproof and windproof.
- Walking socks
- Gloves with a hat

d. Footwear:

- Strong hiking boots
- Socks that wick away moisture
- (Optional for muddy or snowy circumstances) Gaiters

e. Backpack:

- A properly sized backpack
- Waterproof pack liner or rain cover

f. Hydration:

- Hydration reservoirs or water bottles
- Method of water purification (filter, purification tablets)

g. Nutrition:

- Snacks that are high in energy
- Longer treks need portable lunches.
- Cookware and a lightweight stove (for multi-day trips)

h. First Aid Supplies:

- Supplies for basic first aid (bandages, antiseptics, pain medications)
- Treatment of blisters
- Medications on prescription

i. Illumination:

- A flashlight or a headlamp
- Additional batteries

j. Knife or Multitool:

- Knife or multi-tool in a small package

k. Emergency Shelter:

- A space blanket or an emergency bivvy

l. Fire Starter:

- Matches or lighters that are waterproof
- Cotton balls drenched in petroleum jelly (firestarter)

m. Communication:

- Mobile phone fully charged
- Charger on the go

n. Personal Items:

- Sunscreen
- Repellent for insects
- Lip gloss
- Items for personal hygiene (toothbrush, toothpaste, biodegradable soap)

o. Optional Equipment:

- Trekking sticks
- Camera
- Binoculars
- Kit for repairs (duct tape, sewing kit)

Remember to tailor the checklist to your personal needs, taking into account aspects such as weather, route complexity, and length of your excursion.

Clothing Considerations

Choosing the correct hiking apparel is critical for being comfortable and safe in a variety of weather situations. Here are some important factors to consider while choosing and layering clothing:

a. Moisture-Wicking Base Layers:

- To keep perspiration away from the skin and retain comfort, use lightweight, moisture-wicking materials for base layers.

b. Insulating Layers:

- Layers of insulation trap heat to keep you warm. Fleece coats and down vests are both wonderful options.

c. Outer Layers:

- The outer layers are waterproof and windproof, protecting against rain, wind, and low temperatures. To avoid overheating, look for breathable fabrics.

d. Socks for Hiking:

- To avoid blisters and give comfort on lengthy walks, use moisture-wicking and cushioned hiking socks.

e. Footwear:

- Hiking footwear with strong ankle support are required. If you expect damp weather, be sure they are waterproof.

f. Headgear:

- Sun protection is provided by a wide-brimmed hat or cap, while warmth is provided by a beanie or hat in colder weather.

g. Gloves:

- Bring light gloves for sun protection and thicker, insulated gloves for chilly weather.

h. Layering:

- Layering helps you to adapt to shifting weather conditions. Begin with a moisture-wicking base layer, then add insulating layers for warmth, followed by a waterproof upper layer.

i. Consider the Season:

- Dress appropriately for the season. Summer walks demand lightweight and breathable clothing, but winter excursions require greater insulation.

Always check the weather forecast before going on a trek and adapt your attire appropriately.

Backpacking Tips

Efficient packing and sensible backpacking habits help to make trekking more fun and efficient. Here are some key backpacking tips:

a. Pack Weight Distribution:
- To preserve balance and avoid pressure on your back, distribute weight equally in your backpack.

b. Lightweight Equipment:

- To reduce the total weight of your bag, invest in lightweight and compact goods.

c. Essentials at the Top:
- For quick access, keep regularly used things, such as food, drinks, and a map, near the top of your bag.

d. Pack Compression:

- Reduce the amount of your gear by using compression bags or straps to produce a more compact and sturdy load.

e. Prepare a Trash Bag:

- Bring a small trash bag to collect all garbage in accordance with Leave No Trace standards.

f. Organize with Stuff Sacks:

- To organize and preserve your goods, use stuff sacks or waterproof bags, particularly in damp weather.

g. Emergency Essentials:

- Maintain easy access to emergency supplies such as a first-aid kit, light, and emergency shelter.

h. Fit Your Backpack Correctly:

- To avoid pain and strain, make sure your backpack is appropriately adjusted to your body. Adjust straps and hip belts as needed.

i. Leave Non-Essentials at Home:

- Determine the need of each item. To save pack weight, leave non-essential stuff at home.

j. Use Efficient Packing:

- Learn how to pack efficiently. Roll your clothes to conserve space, and position heavier things closer to your back.

k. Research Water Sources:

- To prepare your hydration strategy, be aware of the locations of water sources throughout your journey. Carry extra water to last for longer distances.

l. Check Your Gear Before Every Hike:

- Inspect and repair your equipment on a regular basis. Before each walk, double-check that everything is in functioning condition.

These backpacking ideas will not only lower your burden but will also improve your whole hiking experience by increasing comfort and efficiency on the route.

Leave No Trace Principles

Responsible hiking entails reducing our environmental effect in order to conserve natural areas for future generations. The principles of Leave No Trace give guidelines on ethical outdoor practices:

a. Plan ahead of time and prepare:

- Investigate and organize your journey, taking into account rules, weather conditions, and the effect of your visit.

b. Travel and Camp on Durable Surfaces:

- To avoid soil erosion and to safeguard sensitive ecosystems, stay on designated routes and campsites.

c. Proper Waste Disposal:

- Remove all garbage, including food leftovers and biodegradable objects. Use approved restrooms or bury garbage at least 6 to 8 inches deep in a cathole.

d. Leave What You Find:

- Keep animals, vegetation, and historical or cultural treasures in mind. Natural and cultural elements should be left as they were discovered.

e. Minimize Campfire Impact:

- Instead of creating a fire, use a camp stove to cook. If fires are permitted, keep them small and in designated fire rings. Never leave a blazing fire unattended.

f. Respect Wildlife:

- Avoid approaching or feeding animals from a safe distance. Maintain a safe distance from animals to reduce stress.

g. Be Mindful of Other Visitors:

- Allow others to use the route, be quiet in nature, and respect the privacy of other walkers.

h. Educate Yourself and Others:

- Learn and share the ideals of Leave No Trace. Educate people on appropriate outdoor behaviors to help foster a stewardship culture.

Hikers may enjoy the outdoors while limiting their ecological imprint and contributing to the preservation of natural habitats by sticking to these rules.

In conclusion, careful planning, thoughtful packing, and appropriate outdoor activities all contribute to a safe, happy, and sustainable hiking trip. Whether you're going on a short day walk or a multi-day backpacking trip, carrying the correct gear and adhering to ethical standards ensures that you leave the path with memories and that nature remains undisturbed for others to enjoy.

ACCOMMODATIONS

Camping Options

For those wanting a deeper connection to nature, France has a wide range of camping choices. Outdoor enthusiasts may pick an accommodation option that matches with their taste for adventure and seclusion, from established campgrounds to the attraction of wild camping.

a. Campsites

Hikers and outdoor enthusiasts like to stay at established campsites. These campgrounds provide necessary facilities, making them suited for both beginner and seasoned campers. Campsites in France are conveniently positioned among hiking trails and natural attractions, making them an ideal base for exploring.

Campgrounds give a pleasant and controlled camping experience by providing amenities such as defined tent spaces, water access points, and bathroom facilities. Many campgrounds also include extra facilities such as community cooking areas, showers, and even entertainment opportunities to accommodate a wide range of tastes.

Campgrounds in France vary from primitive sites in nature reserves to more sophisticated grounds with full services. Reservations are strongly advised, particularly during high seasons, to assure a place and a hassle-free camping experience.

b. Regulations for Wild Camping
Wild camping is an option to explore for individuals looking for a more immersive and off-the-beaten-path experience. However, it is important to be informed of and follow the rules regulating wild camping in France.

In general, wild camping is legal in France, however exact rules differ by location. There may be limits or defined places where camping is permitted in national parks and nature reserves. Before going wild camping, it is important to verify local legislation and secure any appropriate licenses.

Hikers should practice Leave No Trace principles while wild camping, respecting the ecosystem and minimizing their influence. Camping at least 200 feet away from lakes and streams is required, as is packing out all garbage and keeping natural and cultural assets undisturbed.

The decision between developed campsites and wild camping is influenced by personal tastes, degree of comfort, and desire for privacy. Both alternatives allow you to immerse yourself in the natural splendor of France, providing one-of-a-kind experiences for outdoor aficionados.

Mountain Refuges and Huts

Mountain huts and refuges provide a unique and traditional kind of lodging for hikers visiting France's hilly areas. These shelters are strategically placed along major hiking trails, offering a rest stop for tired hikers and mountaineers.

Mountain huts, also called as "refuges" in French, are often basic shelters located at high altitudes. They are an important aspect of the mountain infrastructure, providing shelter, food, and a feeling of community among hikers. Hiking in a mountain hut gives a cultural experience, enabling hikers to engage with the region's alpine customs.

Mountain hut facilities vary, but they often contain bunk-style sleeping accommodations, shared eating spaces, and minimal conveniences. Hikers might expect rustic circumstances since these hotels promote utility in a mountain setting.

Reservations are recommended to ensure a space in famous mountain huts, particularly during busy hiking seasons. Keep in aware that some huts only accept cash, and it's critical to understand the hut's unique regulations about meals, sleeping arrangements, and amenities.

Staying in mountain huts is a fantastic opportunity to immerse yourself in French alpine culture, interact with other hikers, and enjoy the breathtaking scenery of the high Alps.

Inns and Hostels

For those who prefer the conveniences of a more traditional lodging, France has a variety of hotels and hostels to suit a variety of budgets and interests. The possibilities range from lovely boutique hotels in ancient villages to budget-friendly hostels in lively cities.

a. Hotels:

France has a plethora of hotels, ranging from luxury institutions to intimate boutique lodgings. Historic towns and cities are peppered with attractive hotels that provide a pleasant and culturally rich stay. Many hotels provide facilities such as on-site restaurants, room service, and concierge services to guests looking for a relaxed and pampered stay.

b. Hostels:
Hostels provide inexpensive lodging choices for tourists, particularly hikers and backpackers visiting France. Hostels are often placed in metropolitan areas and famous tourist areas, making them easily accessible and handy. These establishments usually provide dormitory-style rooms with shared utilities, resulting in a sociable ambiance that appeals to a wide spectrum of guests.

Travelers may find lodgings that fit their interests and budget, whether they choose a hotel or a hostel. Hikers can blend their outdoor excursions with the comfort and conveniences afforded by more conventional kinds of housing because to the flexibility of these alternatives.

Finally, France's different lodgings cater to a wide range of interests, guaranteeing that any tourist, from enthusiastic hikers to those looking for a cultural experience, may find the ideal spot to rest and rejuvenate among the country's stunning landscapes and rich past.

FOOD AND CUISINE

Local Specialties

Exploring France's culinary scene is an enjoyable excursion that extends beyond the renowned baguettes and croissants. Each area has its own specialties, demonstrating the variety and depth of French cuisine. Here's a taste of some of the local delicacies you could discover, ranging from savory entrees to delightful sweets:

a. Ratatouille:

Ratatouille is a vegetable medley dish from the sunny area of Provence. It preserves the essence of Mediterranean tastes by using eggplants, zucchini, bell peppers, onions, and tomatoes. Ratatouille is a celebration of fresh, local vegetables, often seasoned with herbs such as thyme and basil.

b. Bouillabaisse:

Bouillabaisse takes center stage in Marseille, a seaside city. This classic fisherman's stew is made using fresh local fish and shellfish, as well as fragrant herbs. It's a seafood lover's dream, served with rouille (garlic-infused mayonnaise) and symbolizing the region's marine tradition.

c. Aligot:
Aligot is a cozy cuisine from the hilly region of Auvergne that blends mashed potatoes with melted cheese, generally Tomme or Gruyère. The end product is a stretchy, cheesy treat that goes well with a variety of meat recipes. The tastes of mountain cuisine are reflected in Aligot.

d. Tarte Flambée:
Tarte flambée, also known as flammekueche, is a popular dish in Alsace's northeastern area. It's topped with crème fraîche, onions, and bacon and looks like a thin-crust pizza. A balanced mix of textures and tastes is created by the combination of crunchy crust and creamy toppings.

e. Cassoulet:
Cassoulet is a slow-cooked dish from the Languedoc area that includes white beans, pig sausages, and other meats such as duck or lamb. The meal exemplifies the powerful and flavorful cuisine of southern France, which is often served during joyful events.

f. Galette Complète:
Brittany is well-known for its galettes, which are savory buckwheat crepes. The galette complète is a traditional French pastry filled with ham, cheese, and a sunny-side-up egg. It exemplifies the simplicity and delectability of Breton cuisine.

g. Calissons
Calissons are a delicious delight from Aix-en-Provence for individuals with a sweet craving. These almond-shaped confections are made from a smooth paste of candied fruits and almonds that is covered with royal icing. Calissons are a hallmark of

Provençal sweetness and are often served at special events.

h. Cidre:
Cidre (apple cider) is the drink of choice in Normandy. Unlike champagne, cidre from Normandy is a still beverage with a crisp and delicious apple taste. It goes very well with local cheeses and shellfish.

Trail Snacks and Meals
It's important to have nutritional and energy-boosting snacks and meals while hiking in France. Consider these trail-friendly choices for a day walk or a longer trek:

a. Baguette and Cheese:
A tried-and-true mix that's both convenient and tasty. A fresh baguette coupled with local cheeses makes for a filling and energizing snack.

b. Trail Mix:
Combine nuts, seeds, dried fruits, and a touch of chocolate to make your trail mix. It's a handy and adaptable snack that contains a combination of proteins, healthy fats, and carbs.

c. Energy Bars:
Bring a range of energy bars to keep you going on your journey. Look for bars with a healthy mix of carbs, protein, and fats.

d. Dried Fruits:
Dried fruits like apricots, figs, and raisins are great trail snacks since they are light and high in natural sugars.

e. Nut Butter Packets:
Individual nut butter packets (peanut butter, almond butter) are handy and high in healthy fats and protein.

f. Quiche:
Prepared quiches may be divided into parts for a satisfying and tasty trail dinner. For a

great experience, choose a variation with veggies, cheese, or ham.

g. Fruits and vegetables:
Consider long-lasting fruits such as apples, pears, or oranges. They provide hydration as well as important vitamins and minerals.

h. Packets of Instant Oatmeal:
Carry quick oatmeal packets with you for a warm and filling supper. Simply combine with hot water for a quick and satisfying breakfast or snack.

Water Sources and Purification
Staying hydrated when hiking is critical, and knowing water sources and purification procedures is critical for a safe and pleasurable outdoor experience in France.

a. Natural Streams and Springs:
In France, several hiking paths pass by natural springs and streams. While some water sources may seem to be clean, it is

best to treat the water before drinking it to remove any possible impurities.

b. Portable Water Filters:
Bring a portable water filter with you to clean water from natural sources. These filters are lightweight and excellent at eliminating germs and protozoa from drinking water on the trail, assuring safe drinking water.

c. Water Purification Tablets:
Water purification tablets are a small and practical method of water treatment. They are simple to use and offer an efficient method of killing dangerous germs.

d. Boiling Water:
Boiling water is a safe way to assure its safety. Pathogens may be eliminated by boiling water for at least one minute (or more at higher altitudes) if you have a portable burner.

e. Hydration Bladders:
Keeping a hydration bladder or reservoir in your backpack enables for frequent and simple drinking, ensuring regular hydration throughout your trip.

f. Carry Enough Water:
Plan your itinerary and keep the distance between water sources in mind. Carry enough water to meet your hydration requirements, particularly in isolated places where water may be scarce.

g. Keep Up to Date on Water Quality:
For the most up-to-date information on water quality along your route, contact local authorities or trail information centers. Water supplies in certain locations may be seasonal or contaminated.

h. Consider Electrolyte Supplements:
Consider bringing electrolyte pills for longer excursions or in hot weather to restore critical minerals lost via perspiration.

Being aware of water sources, bringing purifying equipment, and being appropriately hydrated are all important components of responsible and safe hiking in France. Hikers may enjoy the scenic views while being safe on the path by learning the local terrain and being prepared.

CULTURAL ETIQUETTE

Nature and Trails Respect

France's natural beauty is a gift that both inhabitants and tourists respect and appreciate. When exploring nature and hiking trails, cultural etiquette that fosters environmental protection and courteous engagement with the natural surroundings is crucial.

a. Leave No Trace:

Adopt the "Leave No Trace" principles, which stress reducing your environmental effect. Leave no trace of your presence, remain on approved pathways, and avoid damaging plants and animals. Respect the ecosystems you meet and tread softly to preserve the natural beauty for future generations.

b. Stick to the Trails:

To prevent trampling delicate plants and harming animal habitats, stick to established pathways. Off-roading may cause soil erosion and upset the delicate balance of ecosystems.

c. Pack Out What You Pack In:
Bring a small trash bag with you and collect everything rubbish, including food leftovers. To keep the trails and natural areas in pristine shape, dispose of rubbish correctly. This involves following appropriate garbage disposal standards in campgrounds.

d. Reduce Noise Pollution:
Reduce noise pollution to enjoy nature's tranquillity. Keep talks at a reasonable level and refrain from playing loud music. This permits other hikers and local creatures to enjoy the peace and quiet of the surroundings.

e. Respect Wildlife:
Keep a safe distance from wildlife and avoid the impulse to approach or feed it. Keep a safe distance to prevent stressing animals

and enabling them to go about their normal habits without being disturbed.

f. Follow Fire Regulations:
Follow fire rules if camping is part of your outdoor activity. Use designated fire rings in locations where fires are allowed, and ensure that all flames are completely extinguished before leaving the campground. In areas where there are fire restrictions, use a portable stove.

g. Educate Yourself:
Take the time to study about the flora and wildlife of the area you're visiting. Understanding local ecology broadens your respect for the environment and enables you to make educated choices that support conservation efforts.

h. Practice Responsible Photography:
Take care while photographing nature's beauty. Avoid trampling plants to achieve the ideal view, and shoot animals from a safe distance using a telephoto lens. In

protected locations, observe any photographic restrictions.

Hikers contribute to the preservation of France's unique landscapes by taking a conscious and respectful attitude to nature, ensuring that these natural beauties stay unspoiled for future generations.

Interacting with Residents

France is known for its rich cultural legacy and kind people. Embracing cultural etiquette while dealing with locals develops good ties and improves the travel experience. Here are some crucial points to remember while interacting respectfully:

a. Learn basic French phrases:
While English is often spoken in tourist regions, acquiring a few basic French phrases demonstrates a genuine desire to communicate with people. Simple greetings, thank gestures, and courteous statements go a long way toward building great connections.

b. Respect Personal Space:
Personal space is valued in French society, and it is normal to keep a comfortable distance during interactions. Personal boundaries should be respected, particularly in busy or public locations.

c. Politeness and Greetings:
Begin talks with a formal greeting like "Bonjour" (Good morning) or "Bonsoir" (Good evening). To express politeness, use "s'il vous plaît" (please) and "merci" (thank you). These actions help to create a pleasant and polite encounter.

d. Dress Modestly:
Consider dressed modestly in more formal or religious occasions to respect local norms. This is especially important while visiting churches, cathedrals, or attending cultural events.

e. Dining Etiquette:
When eating out, follow the local dining etiquette. Keep your hands on the table

throughout meals and wait for the host or hostess to signal where you should seat. As a token of thanks, use acceptable utensils and eat your whole dish.

f. Use "Vous" and "Tu" Correctly:
The formal and informal forms of address in French are "vous" and "tu" correspondingly. Use "vous" when addressing strangers, elderly, or in professional contexts. The use of "tu" indicates a more intimate, informal connection.

g. Be Punctual:
In French culture, punctuality is highly prized. Be on time whether meeting locals for a guided tour or attending a social gathering. It demonstrates kindness and consideration for the schedules of others.

h. Respect Social Customs:
Learn about local customs and traditions, particularly if you live in a rural or small-town location. Participating in local festivals or events, for example, allows you

to interact with the community and learn about cultural customs directly.

Respecting local traditions and acting politely and considerately improves cultural interchange between tourists and residents, generating good ties and a greater awareness for the distinctive characteristics of French culture.

Trail Rules and Etiquette

When exploring France's hiking trails, following trail etiquette and following set standards contributes to a safe and pleasurable experience for everybody. The following are important criteria for appropriate trail behavior:

a. Yielding on Trails:

Follow the designated trail yielding rules. Hikers heading uphill have the right of way in most cases. Allow people to pass safely by being polite and stepping aside.

b. Stay on Designated Trails:
Off-trail travel may cause soil erosion, damage to plants, and disturbance of animal habitats. To reduce your environmental effect, always remain on specified trails.

c. Hiking in Single File:
When pathways get narrow or meet additional hikers, switch to single-file trekking to enable everyone to pass safely. This is particularly crucial on small or steep path sections.

d. Respect Trail Closures:
Keep an eye out for trail closures and limitations. These restrictions may be in place to safeguard sensitive ecosystems, species, or to protect the environment during times of ecological fragility. Respecting closures helps conservation efforts.

e. Remove All Waste:
Pack away all rubbish in a "Leave No Trace" manner. This covers not simply food wrappers, but any biodegradable garbage as

well. When available, use appropriate garbage receptacles.

f. Reduce Noise Levels:
On the path, have a calm and courteous manner. Avoid listening to loud music and conduct talks at a level that does not disrupt the natural environment or other hikers.

g. Control Pets:
Keep dogs on a leash and under control while hiking with them. Make certain that your dogs do not disturb animals or other hikers. Clean up after your dogs and dispose of their trash.

h. Respect Wildlife:
Observe wildlife from a safe distance and avoid approaching or feeding animals. This protects the indigenous species and allows for more genuine animal behavior.

i. Keep Local Regulations in Mind:
Learn about local trail laws, including any restrictions on camping, fires, or off-trail exploring. Following these rules encourages a happy coexistence of hikers and the environment.

j. Emergency Planning:
Prepare for crises by keeping necessary materials on hand, such as a first-aid kit, a map, and communication gadgets. Inform someone of your hiking intentions and projected return time, particularly if the path is isolated or difficult.

k. Educate Other Hikers:
Share trail etiquette standards with your fellow hikers, particularly those who are new to responsible hiking. Raising awareness helps to build a community of ecologically informed and thoughtful trail users.

Hikers play an important part in protecting the integrity of hiking trails, providing a good experience for everyone, and conserving the natural beauty that makes France a sought-after destination for outdoor lovers by adopting trail etiquette and respecting set guidelines.

RESOURCES AND APPLICATIONS

Topographical Maps

Exploring France's various landscapes requires dependable navigation aids, and topographic maps remain an essential resource for hikers. These thorough maps provide a plethora of information that will help travelers comprehend the terrain, plan itineraries, and navigate with confidence. Here's a detailed look at the value of topographic maps for hiking in France:

a. How to Read Topographic Maps:

Topographic maps are precise depictions of a terrain that illustrate elevation contours, rivers, lakes, forests, and pathways. These maps employ contour lines to show the form and height of the terrain, allowing hikers to perceive the three-dimensional qualities of the area.

b. Elevation Contours:
Topographic maps use contour lines to show elevation variations. Hikers can evaluate the steepness of slopes, locate valleys and peaks, and plan routes that are appropriate for their fitness and skill levels by attentively inspecting these lines.

c. Information about the trail:
Marked trails on topographic maps assist hikers in navigating existing routes and discovering new pathways. Trail symbols and distance markers help hikers plan the length and difficulty of their journeys.

d. Identification of Landforms:
Hikers may recognize noteworthy features such as peaks, plateaus, and canyons by studying the map. This information improves the hiking experience overall by offering a greater grasp of the geographical aspects experienced.

e. Emergency Navigation:
Topographic charts are important for navigation in the case of unforeseen changes or crises. Hikers may find alternate routes, water supplies, and the vicinity of adjacent landmarks or civilization.

f. GPS Device Compatibility:
Many topographic maps are GPS-compatible, enabling hikers to combine contemporary technology with conventional navigation methods. This combination improves accuracy while also providing real-time position monitoring.

g. Map Legends:
Understanding the legend of the map is critical. Legends decipher map symbols, explaining the significance of contour lines, trail markers, and other cartographic components. This information guarantees that the map is correctly interpreted.

h. Recommended Topographic Maps for France:

IGN (Institut national de l'information géographique et forestière): France's official mapping organization creates precise topographic maps of the whole country. The 1:25,000 scale IGN maps are very popular for hiking since they include all routes and terrain.

i. Map Accessories:

For conventional navigation, topographic maps should be supplemented by a compass. Waterproof map covers also protect maps from the weather, ensuring they stay legible and undamaged while hiking.

j. Digital Topographic Maps:

Aside from traditional maps, numerous applications and websites provide digital topographic maps. These digital versions often include interactive capabilities, such as zooming in and out, switching between various map layers, and planning routes more dynamically.

In essence, topographic maps are a must-have tool for hikers in France, providing a wealth of information for both planning and navigating the trip. Adventurers may start on travels with a heightened feeling of awareness and appreciation for the places they traverse by learning the interpretation of these maps.

Hiking Apps

Hiking applications have become vital companions for outdoor lovers in the digital age, offering a variety of functions that improve the whole hiking experience. These applications are essential tools for hikers experiencing France's different terrains, whether aiding with navigation, measuring fitness, or exchanging trail observations. Here's a more in-depth look at the relevance of hiking apps:

a. GPS Navigation:
Hiking applications with GPS capabilities provide real-time navigation, enabling users to monitor their whereabouts, plan

itineraries, and precisely follow trails. Apps such as Gaia GPS and AllTrails provide sophisticated mapping tools that work in tandem with GPS technology.

b. Offline Maps:
Many hiking applications enable users to save maps for offline usage. This is especially useful in locations with poor or no cellphone service, allowing hikers to use maps even when they are not connected to the internet.

c. Trail Information:
Hiking applications compile large databases of routes and provide information such as path length, elevation gain, difficulty ratings, and user reviews. Hikers may use this information to choose paths that suit their tastes and ability levels.

d. Statistics and Tracking:
Hiking applications with fitness monitoring capabilities collect important facts such as distance traveled, elevation gain, and speed.

Hikers may use this data to measure their progress, create fitness goals, and track their development over time.

e. Offline Trail Recording:
ViewRanger and Komoot are apps that allow users to record their treks and share the GPS tracks with the community. This feature not only keeps a personal record of your hiking trips, but it also offers useful trail information to the app's user community.

f. Safety Features:
Some hiking applications include features like real-time location sharing with selected contacts, emergency SOS functionality, and weather updates. These features improve hiker safety and give peace of mind when out on the trail.

g. Geotagging and Photo Sharing:
Hikers may record their adventures by geotagging images from inside the app. This generates a visual record of the hike and enables users to share their experiences with

other app users or on social networking channels.

h. Community and Reviews:
Hiking applications build a feeling of community by enabling users to share their adventures, tips, and thoughts. Reading evaluations and recommendations from other hikers improves trip planning and aids in the discovery of hidden treasures in the French outdoors.

i. Recommended Hiking Apps for France:

- AllTrails: Provides an enormous trail database with user reviews and images.
- Gaia GPS is well-known for its comprehensive maps and offline navigation features.
- ViewRanger: Offline mapping, trail recording, and a network of outdoor enthusiasts are all available with ViewRanger.

- Komoot: Provides trip planning, offline maps, and user-generated information.

j. Device Compatibility:
Hiking applications work with a variety of devices, including smartphones and wearables. Check that your selected app is compatible with your desired device and that it has enough battery life to last the length of your journey.

Hiking applications have transformed how hikers plan, navigate, and share their outdoor adventures. These applications improve as technology advances, delivering an ever-expanding assortment of capabilities to enhance the fun and safety of hiking experiences in France.

Useful Websites
Using excellent websites devoted to outdoor lovers, you may navigate the plethora of information accessible for hiking in France. These platforms include a wide range of

services, including trail information and trip planning tools, as well as community forums and safety recommendations. Let us investigate the relevance of these websites:

a. Trail Planning and Information:
Hikers in France may get precise topographic maps and trail information from websites like IGN (Institut national de l'information géographique et forestière). Trail descriptions, difficulty ratings, and elevation profiles are available to users, allowing for more extensive trip planning.

b. Weather Prediction:
It is important to check the weather forecast before going trekking. Météo-France, for example, provides precise and up-to-date meteorological information for particular locations, enabling hikers to plan their journeys with weather in mind.

c. Hiking Organizations:
Hikers may benefit from the resources provided by national and regional hiking

groups. The French Federation of Hiking (FFRandonnée) is a fantastic resource for hiking paths, safety requirements, and planned activities.

d. Accommodation Booking:
Booking.com and Airbnb make it easy to reserve lodging, whether hikers prefer hotels, hostels, or vacation rentals. These platforms provide a variety of possibilities for various budgets and tastes.

e. Travel Forums and Communities:
Hikers may seek advice, exchange stories, and connect with other outdoor enthusiasts by joining online travel forums and communities such as Lonely Planet's Thorn Tree or Reddit's r/hiking. These venues are useful for learning from individuals who have traveled similar paths.

f. Safety and Regulations:
Government agencies and hiking groups' websites offer safety standards and laws for certain locations. Understanding these

standards ensures that hikers may enjoy the trails in a responsible and legal manner.

g. Trip Reports and Blogs:

Reading other hikers' trip reports and blogs gives firsthand information of trail conditions, scenic highlights, and problems. Camino de Santiago Forums and personal hiking blogs provide personal opinions that might be useful for trip preparation.

h. Regional Tourism Websites:

Regional tourism websites, such as those devoted to certain departments or provinces, provide information on local attractions, cultural events, and other outdoor activities. These websites give a comprehensive overview of the areas hikers want to visit.

i. Language Resources:

Hikers who are not proficient in French might use language study apps like Duolingo or Babbel to improve conversation and cultural immersion while hiking.

j. Travel Insurance Providers:

Reputable travel insurance companies' websites, such as World Nomads or Allianz Travel, give crucial information about travel insurance coverage. Hikers should make certain that they have enough covering for their outdoor activities.

Finally, handy websites play an important part in streamlining the planning process for hiking experiences in France. These online services provide hikers with the knowledge they need to make educated choices and have a seamless outdoor experience in France's gorgeous landscapes, from trail information to weather predictions and community interaction.

EMERGENCY PREPAREDNESS

First-Aid Kits

Emergency planning is necessary while traveling France's many landscapes. Hikers who carry a well-stocked first aid kit may respond quickly to minor injuries or unanticipated situations. Here's a detailed guide on assembling a hiking first aid kit:

a. Basic Supplies:

- Bandages with adhesive (various sizes)
- Sterile gauze pads with adhesive tape
- Antiseptic wipes or solution
- Splinters and ticks are removed using tweezers.
- scissors for cutting bandages and tape
- Gloves that may be thrown away
- Pain relievers (like acetaminophen and ibuprofen)

- Antihistamines are medications used to treat allergic reactions.

b. Wound Care:

- Sterile wound dressings and nonstick pads
- Elastic bandages and compression wraps
- Moleskin or blister pads for feet
- Antibacterial ointment
- Itching and rashes are treated with hydrocortisone cream.

c. Tools and Instruments:

- A thermometer, a digital face shield, an emergency siren, a multi-tool, or a knife
- This little flashlight comes with extra batteries.
- Ice packs that melt instantly

d. Medications:

- Prescription medication (if necessary)
- Medication accessible without a prescription for nausea, diarrhea, and motion sickness.
- Any personal medications that are required

e. Personal Items:

- Medical history and contact details in case of an emergency
- Health insurance information
- Photocopies of identification (passport, driver's license)
- Notepad with pen

f. Special Considerations:

- Use an EpiPen or other prescription emergency medication if required.
- Emergency blanket or space blanket
- Hand sanitizer or sanitizing wipes

g. Storage:

- Keep the first aid kit in a waterproof and durable container or bag to protect it from the elements.
- Regularly check and replace supplies to ensure the kit is always ready to use.

h. Training:

- Hikers should be familiar with the contents and use of the first aid kit.
- Consider taking a basic first aid and CPR course to boost your preparedness.

Emergency Contact Information

A list of emergency contacts is an essential aspect of hiking preparedness. Having contact information easily accessible in the case of an emergency encourages fast communication and help. Here's how to make an emergency contact list step by step:

a. Local Emergency Services:

- Know the emergency phone number for the region you're trekking in. In France, dial 112 for an emergency.
- Look for the contact information for your local police, medical services, and search and rescue agencies.

b. Personal Emergency Contacts:

- Include contact information for family members, friends, or colleagues who should be called if an emergency occurs.
- Describe your connection to the contact person (spouse, parent, close friend, etc.).

c. Medical Professionals:

- Include contact information for your primary care doctor and any specialists you visit on a regular basis.

- Include your desired hospital or medical facility's phone number and address.

d. Travel Insurance Provider:

- Include the contact information for your travel insurance provider.
- Learn about the coverage details and claim filing methods.

e. Consulate/Embassy:

- If you are a foreign traveler, provide the contact information for your country's embassy or consulate in France.

f. Group Members:

- If hiking in a group, exchange emergency contact information with your fellow hikers.
- Make a copy of the list of emergency contacts for each member.

g. Communication Devices:

- Carry a fully charged phone with emergency contact information with you at all times.
- Consider employing communication equipment such as two-way radios or satellite phones in places where cellular service is weak.

Search and Rescue Information

Hikers, particularly those venturing into isolated or challenging terrain, must be informed of search and rescue information. Understanding the available processes and resources may help to speed aid in times of need. A hiker's guide to search and rescue information is available here:

a. Local Search and Rescue (SAR) Organizations:

- Investigate and preserve the contact information for local search and rescue groups in the hiking region.

- Discover their expertise and the services they provide.

b. Emergency Warning Signs:

- As an emergency beacon, consider carrying a personal locator beacon (PLB) or a satellite messenger device.
- Make sure you register the equipment with the right authorities and that you understand how to operate it.

c. Trailhead Information:

Before undertaking a trek, check the trailhead for information on emergency protocols and contact information for local authorities.

d. Hiking Permits and Regulations:

- Look for any hiking permits or rules in the region you're visiting.
- Understand the consequences of breaking the rules, since they may

have an influence on search and rescue response.

e. Informing Others of Your Plans:

- Leave a thorough itinerary, including your intended route, projected return time, and any other routes, with a trustworthy person.
- In the case of a delay or an emergency, this information will help search and rescue crews locate you.

f. International SOS:

- Keep the contact information for International SOS or any worldwide help group ready.

g. Satellite Communication:

- Consider carrying a satellite communication device for emergency communication in locations where cellphone service is restricted or non-existent.

h. Stay Calm and Follow Instructions:

- In the case of an emergency, remain calm and obey any directions issued by local authorities or search and rescue personnel.
- Clear communication is essential, as is providing relevant information about your location and circumstances.

i. Helicopter Evacuation:

- Be warned that helicopter evacuation may be required in distant places.
- Follow the directions given by rescue crews for safe evacuation methods.

j. Communication Channels:

- Listen to approved emergency communication channels on radios or gadgets if provided by local authorities.

Hiking in new terrain is always dangerous, and being prepared for emergencies is a wise strategy. Hikers may enjoy their outdoor activities with better safety and confidence if they prepare a well-stocked first aid pack, have an emergency contact list, and learn search and rescue methods.

CONCLUSION

Hiking in the wide and beautiful landscapes of France is a voyage of discovery, adventure, and intimate connection with nature. This thorough guide has sought to offer you with the information and tools you need to guarantee that your hiking experience in France is not only entertaining but also safe and well-prepared.

Immerse yourself in the rich cultural tapestry that follows you as you cross the varied terrains, from the magnificent French Alps to the beautiful coastline paths and the gorgeous wine area. France's historical trails and pathways provide both a cultural and physical adventure, enabling you to observe the history inscribed into the very fabric of the country.

Visa needs, health and safety measures, currency concerns, and transportation knowledge all help you get to the heart of your hiking journey with ease. Top hiking areas like the French Alps and Pyrenees await exploration, each presenting a unique tapestry of obstacles and spectacular panoramas. On coastal paths, the rhythmic symphony of waves calls, while wine region treks provide a sensory combination of gorgeous scenery and excellent tastes.

This book goes into path difficulty levels, offering a nuanced perspective and alternatives for hikers of all abilities, including beginners, intermediates, and seasoned hikers. Using the path responsibly and respecting both nature and local traditions adds to the authenticity of your adventure, promoting a happy interaction between the explorer and the explored.

In the spirit of total readiness, the book dives into emergency issues, highlighting the significance of a well-stocked first aid bag, a rigorously maintained list of emergency contacts, and a grasp of search and rescue processes. These components work together to construct a safety net, enabling you to confidently manage the unexpected with knowledge and resources.

Consider the route a transforming passage, one that, as you start out, stitches the tapestry of your trip with strands of culture, history, and the pure beauty of the French wilderness. This book is intended to be both a companion and a resource, ensuring that your feet echo the rhythm of the French landscapes and your heart beats in sync with the pulse of the trails.

May your hiking vacation to France be a symphony of discovery, cultural enrichment, and personal achievements, leaving unforgettable images on your wanderlust canvas. Best wishes, and may the paths reveal new vistas under your eager feet.

Printed in Great Britain
by Amazon

59425661R00076